For Bereaved Grandparents

By Margaret H. Gerner

Original Illustrations by Glenda Dietrich

Design by Janet Sieff, Centering Corporation

Revised 2004

ISBN: 1-56123-002-2

Centering Corporation is a small, non-profit bereavement resource center.
Please call or write for a free catalog of available material.

Centering Corporation
Omaha, NE 68104

This little book is dedicated to:

My beautiful son, Arthur
My precious granddaughter, Emily
And
Robbie, Christine, Jessica, Erica, Matthew Jr., Julie, David Jr.,
And my grandchildren yet to be born

GRIEF

I am powerlessness. I am helplessness. I am frustration. I sit with her and I cry with her. She cries for her daughter and I cry for mine. I can't help her. I can't reach inside her and take her broken heart. I must watch her suffer day after day.

I listen to her tell me over and over how she misses Emily, how she wants her back. I can't bring Emily back for her. I can't buy her an even better Emily than she had, like I could buy her an even better toy when she was a child. I can't kiss the hurt and make it go away. I can't even kiss a small part of it away. There's no band-aid large enough to cover her bleeding heart.

There was a time I could listen to her talk about a fickle boyfriend and tell her it would be okay, and know in my heart that in two weeks she wouldn't even think of him. Can I tell her it'll be okay in two years when I know it will never be okay, that she will carry this pain of "what might have been" in her deepest heart for the rest of her life?

I see this young woman, my child, who was once carefree and fun loving and bubbling with life, slumped in a chair with her eyes full of agony. Where is my power now? Where is my mother's bag of tricks that will make it all better?

Why can't I join her in the aloneness of her grief? As tight as my arms wrap around her, I can't reach that aloneness.

What can I give her to make her better? A cold, wet cloth will ease the swelling of her crying eyes, but it won't stop the reason for her tears. What treat will bring joy back to her? What prize will bring that happy child smile back? Where are the magic words to give her comfort? What chapter in Dr. Spock tells me how to do this? He has told me everything else I've needed to know.

Where are the answers? I should have them. I'm the mother.

I know that someday she'll find happiness again, that her life will have meaning again. I can hold out hope for her someday, but what about now? This minute? This hour? This day?

I can give her my love and my prayers and my care and my concern. I could give her my life. But even that won't help.

I wrote this piece out of deep feelings of powerlessness. It seemed that no matter what I did, I could not take away my daughter's pain at the death of her three-year-old daughter, Emily. Were that not enough, I was devastated by my own grief at the loss of my precious granddaughter.

I could relate to my daughter's pain. I, too, had lost a child. In 1971 my six-year-old son, Arthur, was killed by an automobile. At that time there were no support groups. I didn't know how to grieve or that what I was feeling was normal. I thought I was losing my mind. The psychiatrist I saw after Arthur's death reinforced my belief by giving me drugs for my "depression."

I tried to do what people told me to do; count my blessings and be "strong." That meant not talking about Arthur, not crying, and not expressing any other emotions I felt. The result was five years of distorted, prolonged grief which eventually had to be resolved with the help of a professional who had training in bereavement.

When my daughter lost her child – that very day in the hospital, with Emily growing cold under my hands – I swore this would not happen to Dorothy. I didn't know how, but I knew I was going to do everything possible to help her. I knew what she had ahead of her.

I was shattered by Emily's death, but my grief lessened sooner than Dorothy's. Since Emily was not my child, I recovered many months ahead of my daughter. What didn't lessen was seeing Dorothy's pain. That continues, at times, even today.

As a parent of a grieving child, you have a unique opportunity to cement a deep and lasting relationship with your child.

You have the opportunity to walk with your child through the most difficult life experience he or she will ever endure.

You have the opportunity to help your child in a very special way, and the bond that forms will never be broken.

It will not be easy, and the process is long and hard. You will feel powerless, frustrated and helpless many times.

But you CAN help.

Grandparent grief is like a fork with two tines. One tine represents the loss of a grandchild, and the other represents the pain of seeing your own child suffer. Therefore, you have two tasks. The first is to work through your own grief, and the other is to feel helpful to your bereaved child. There may be two parts, but you actually deal with them at the same time.

The first tine of grandparent grief is your own grief over the loss of a precious grandchild.

Grief is the normal reaction to a loss. Actually, we experience grief throughout our lives. A pet dies. A friend moves away. Our children go off to college. We lose a job. We grieve these losses, but we don't always realize that's what we are doing. With a grandchild's death, we face one of life's most painful griefs.

The danger in listing the manifestations of grief is that we tend to think we should fit into certain patterns. If we don't experience them like "the book" says, we think something is wrong with us. Don't fall into that trap. Many things determine how you grieve. We are all individuals in our personalities, experiences, ways of coping, and grief timetables. Your feelings will be the same as those of many other grandparents. At the same time, your grief and feelings will be uniquely and singularly yours. The following are some typical grief manifestations:

Denial – When you heard your grandchild was dead you probably denied it. "Oh, No!," you may have said, even if the child died after a long illness. Denial is a protective mechanism that cushions the mental blow.

Shock – Along with denial, shock sets in almost immediately. The knowledge that your grandchild has died is almost impossible to face, so your mind attempts to shut off that reality. It is as though your mind says, "This is too painful. I'll put it off for a while."

Each of us reacts to shock differently. Some of us mentally and emotionally withdraw from everything, doing only what we are told. Some of us participate but with little feeling. Still others of us are totally disabled and can do no more than attend the funeral. Most of us react with some combination of these.

When shock leaves, the reality of death hits. Frequently, you will hear a griever say, "I was doing so well. Now, all at once, I'm miserable." This is what happens: shock numbs us to the pain for a time, and then – the real pain beings. When this happens you may have appetite problems or difficulty sleeping. You may be obsessed with thoughts of your grandchild and want to talk about details of the death over and over.

You may cry incessantly and have trouble concentrating. You may experience fatigue and even physical pain. You may experience extreme guilt or anger. All these feelings are normal. Let's talk about each of them separately.

Sleep Problems – Most bereaved grandparents find sleep difficult for a time. When you can't sleep, it may be helpful to try warm milk or a bath before bed, reading, using relaxation techniques or relaxation tapes, or keeping a notebook by the bed to write out feelings and thoughts. Don't fight sleeplessness. Accept the fact that this is normal and temporary, and the rest you get by lying quietly can be almost as helpful as sleep. Be careful of drugs or alcohol. Neither produces normal sleep, and they may even delay your healing.

Appetite Changes – A grieving person is seldom concerned with nutrition or a well-balanced diet, but proper nutrition is more important now than ever before. The quantity of food is not vital, but the quality is. Include something from the four food groups (milk, meat, fruit/vegetable, grain) in each meal. Water, too, is important. Drink at least eight medium-size glasses of water each day. You may want to pour eight glasses into a pitcher and be sure you drink it all during the day. Avoid caffeine and alcohol. It's also a good idea to take a good, general vitamin daily.

Adequate sleep and good nutrition are especially important for us because we're older. We don't have the physical resilience that our bereaved children have.

Constant Thoughts – In the early weeks, you may think about your grandchild, the death and your bereaved child almost constantly. This is not unusual. It's your mind's way of sorting out what happened. Let yourself think. Contrary to what people might tell you, you are not "dwelling" on painful thoughts, you are processing. This will lessen as you begin to heal.

Constant Talk – You need to hear yourself say, out loud, what you are thinking and feeling. This helps you see the reality of the death. Talking about your grandchild, your feelings and the death is the most healing thing you can do. The problem is finding someone to listen to you. Your friends are likely to tell you it's not good to talk about these things. Others may simply be uncomfortable listening to your pain. No matter! Find someone who will let you talk. It is necessary for you to talk. Talking with your bereaved child helps both of you.

Some grandparents report talking to anyone who will listen, even total strangers. Some find that talking into a tape recorder helps. Some talk out loud to themselves. Others find it helpful to write to their grandchild who died, saying goodbye and sharing their feelings. However you do it, remember, *talking is essential.*

Crying – The death of a grandchild can cause extreme physical and emotional stress. This stress must be released periodically. Crying is an effective way to do that. The more energy you can release by crying, the healthier you will be, both physically and emotionally. Release of this emotional energy explains why you feel better after a good cry.

Crying can do so much to help us heal, but unfortunately most of us have been brought up with the idea that tears are a sign of weakness. Let go of that idea! Let yourself cry! You have every right!

Some people say, *"If I ever let myself start crying, I'll never stop."* Yes, you will. Crying is self-terminating, and because it expends so much energy, you'll usually feel exhausted after a session of hard crying. You may even rest better. Remember, crying is not "breaking down." Crying is a gentle melting that lets the pain flow out of you.

Inability to Concentrate – This part of grief can be very disconcerting and uncomfortable. You may feel confused or as if your thought processes have slowed down. You may find yourself in the grocery store staring for five minutes at the peas and carrots, forgetting which you were going to get. Some people feel this confusion for many months, while others experience little of it. Again, we are all different.

You can handle the inability to concentrate in different ways. Muddle through it, write yourself detailed instructions or reminder notes, and eliminate as many jobs as you can. If you can accept this reaction as normal and temporary, you will be less bothered by it.

Anger – Most people feel angry after a death. You may be angry at God, life, the doctor or any person you hold responsible for your grandchild's death. You may even feel anger towards your own child for "letting this happen." Anger isn't always rational, but nonetheless it's there and must be faced.

Grandmothers, especially, have been raised with the idea that it's not acceptable to express anger. If this is true for you, a good suggestion is to write out your anger. In a letter, or a notebook, pour out all the bitterness, frustration (and yes, even hatred) you feel. Pour out all the venom raging inside you. Periodically read over it, and if you continue to feel anger, add to what you have already written. Eventually, you will have vented your feelings. When you're no longer angry, tear up what you have written and throw it away. One grandmother felt guilty when she was angry at God for not preventing her granddaughter's sudden death. Her pastor reminded her that, "God could take it." Sometimes an angry prayer is the most honest and real prayer we can pray.

Guilt – Most of us experience guilt. If there's no real guilt, we'll manufacture some. Because this is such a difficult problem, we have devoted a special section to it. For now, we'll just say that guilt is a normal part of the grief process.

Your Body Grieves, Too – Physical problems such as weakness, fatigue, infections, colds, stomach problems, increased blood pressure and headaches are common to bereaved grandparents. Any chronic physical ailments you already have can be aggravated now. It's important to have a check-up, but be sure your physician knows you are grieving and understands that grief is normal. It's a part of life, not a pathological or emotional illness. Unfortunately, many doctors still see grief as "sick," and will prescribe medication to lessen your physical problems. Just be extremely careful of allowing any doctor to try to alleviate the stress of your grief with mind or mood-altering chemicals.

Your reaction to your grandchild's death is likely to be different from that of your spouse or the other set of grandparents. Don't compare yourself with them or think something is wrong with you if you grieve differently. Many things in our personalities, cultures, religions, and lives contribute to how we grieve. We hope you take the suggestions here and allow yourself to openly express your emotions. It isn't easy to change old patterns, but try. You can't avoid or bury grief. You must go through it. Sadness must be expressed through tears. Anger and guilt must be talked out and looked at honestly. Lean into the pain and allow yourself to experience it. In other words, allow yourself to be miserable when you need to be. This is what "working through" grief means.

HELPING YOUR GRIEVING CHILD

One grandmother told me: *"Timmie's death is tearing me up, but seeing my daughter, Terry, in such pain is much worse. She is so different. The sadness I see in her eyes haunts me. Nothing pleases her. She's not interested in anything. All she does is talk about Timmie. She tells me she just wants to die so she can be with him. She cries and cries and there isn't a thing I can do to make it better for her. I don't know what I'm going to do."*

I felt like Timmie's grandmother. While I knew what Dorothy's needs were, and I tried to meet them every way I could, there were times I doubted that anything I did helped. I wanted to "kiss it and make it better," and I wanted her better now. Without a moment's hesitation, I would have gladly taken her pain myself. I missed my precious Emily, but the feelings of helplessness around Dorothy's pain were even greater.

This is the hardest part of being a bereaved grandparent. There will be times you feel that nothing you do makes a difference. You will think your child will never "get over" this. But remember, the grief will not always be as intense and devastating as it is today, and your help will be forever appreciated.

The most important thing you can do is to understand your child's grief. This is essential. Read **The Bereaved Parent**, by Harriet Schiff. This book will help you understand this unique, intense grief, and will assure you that your child is not emotionally ill. Remember, there is no grief exactly like that which comes with the loss of a child.

There are several factors that make parental grief unique:

Loss of Part of Self – The parent/child relationship is the most intense that life can generate. The child was literally a part of the parent at one time. When you lose a child, you lose part of yourself.

Loss of Meaning – Children give direction to life. Rearing and providing for them becomes a primary goal. With a child's death, even if there are other children, this goal changes. Life seems meaningless.

Loss of Support – Expectations are that parents will lean on each other and support each other. Parents themselves expect this, but it rarely happens. Each parent is so debilitated by grief that neither has the energy to support the other. One mother said, "It's impossible to lean on a tree that is already bending." Loss of support takes many forms.

Different grieving styles can create problems in a relationship. One may grieve openly, with much expression. The other may grieve inwardly and quietly. It is difficult for parents with opposite coping styles to respect the other's way of grieving. The inward-griever doesn't want to see the constant crying and lamenting of the other. The open-griever doesn't think the other one cares or has feelings. This leads to wrong assumptions and misinterpretation of feelings.

Guilt and blame can also prevent support. One may blame the other for real or imagined wrongs. The one blamed may withdraw with intense guilt feelings. This can create a wedge that may take professional help to resolve, especially if, in fact, one was somehow involved in the death.

Parental resemblance is very common. Frequently a child and parent look very much alike. This can be difficult for the other parent. Seeing the child's face or mannerisms daily, yet knowing that the child is not alive, is constantly painful. For the other parent, just looking in a mirror can bring tears of hurt and recognition.

Changes in sexual activities can create problems, too. One may want the warmth and intimacy that intercourse gives them, while the other may suddenly find sex repulsive.

Loss of Identity – When a child is born, parents take on the identify of parent. When that identity is thwarted by the child's death, they are hit at the most basic level. They lose the sense of "who they are." They must give up parenting the child who died, but continue parenting any surviving children. They must give up being parents and remain parents at the same time. This can create extreme internal conflicts.

The Myth of Perfect Parenthood – Most parents believe that they should care for their children and protect them from harm at all costs. Society also expects that parents will never let anything happen to their children. When a child dies, parents feel that they have failed.

Length of Parental Grief – The many psychological tasks of parental grief take considerable time to work through, therefore a parent may grieve intensely for well over two years. It is not uncommon for parents to grieve even into five years or more, and their child is never forgotten. Often they are denied the support of others who accuse them of hanging on to grief too long.

Keep these unique characteristics of parental grief in mind, especially if you begin to compare your grief over your grandchild's death or your other past losses with how your child is feeling. To get through grief takes considerable emotional work over a long period of time. It's because of these special factors that your bereaved child's grief will last longer and be more intense than yours.

WHAT WE
CAN DO

Encourage Talking – Like you, bereaved parents have a strong need to talk about what they think and feel. Encourage talking. Never say, "You shouldn't say that." Allow them to talk about their child and about their child's death.

Allow Your Child to Cry – Crying, even sobbing, is healthy and necessary. Repressed tears can leads to a host of physical ailments. Tears are helpful in letting out the pain and releasing pent up stress. Never say, "Control yourself." Avoid worrying about what other people will think if your child cries in front of them. Your child is not there to take care of others. Remember, this bout of crying will pass, and while it may disturb you for a while, your child will feel better. Crying with your child can be therapeutic for both of you.

Talk About Your Grandchild – Don't worry that it will make your child cry. You don't remind her of her child. He is on her mind most of the time, anyway. Talking about the child tells her you care. If she cries, she is crying because her child is dead, not because you brought it up. Actually, the tears you may help to precipitate can be good for her.

Listen to Your Bereaved Child – The greatest gift you can give your child is a listen. It is so important, and so difficult sometimes, that we've included a separate section on how to listen.

Few bereaved parents have someone who will listen to stories about their child or about how guilty or angry they feel. You can be that listener. Even if you have not had open communication with your child up to now, you can change that. One of the most talked-about subjects in groups of young bereaved parents is the lack of understanding from their parents. If you really listen, you'll understand. Your child needs you to listen and needs you terribly.

Use non-judgmental listening. Our generation has been taught to "control" ourselves, to keep feelings inside, that the person who doesn't talk about the loss of a loved one and who doesn't cry is doing "well." These ideas are wrong, and certainly not helpful. We now know that suppressed grief is unhealthy, both emotionally and physically.

At the same time, we have been taught to love, to help others, to grow and adjust. We've been taught to be creative and try new things. You can use these positive teachings in listening to and loving your child.

In addition to sadness and loss, your child will probably feel **guilt.** In most cases the guilt is irrational, but putting it into words helps your child realize it is illogical or simply wears the guilt out. You may be able to help her see she did the best she could with the knowledge she had at the time, but in early grief, simply listening is the most helpful. Never say, "Don't feel guilty." She must come to see that herself. If you point out too soon that the guilt is illogical, it may seem that you are saying, "Don't feel." This may cause your child to keep all feelings inside.

Your child may also experience **anger.** Anger may be directed anywhere at the doctor, the hospital, God, or even the dead child. Anger, too, may be illogical, but the emotion is there and needs to be verbalized. Allow your child to talk about who or what generates the anger. Listen to all the dire threats and thoughts. It's a good way of getting out the tension behind the anger. Rarely do parents carry out threats. Allowing them to talk about anger will diffuse it. If you feel you and your child need some physical activity to "pound" the anger out, take a walk together, hit a bed with a dish towel, or buy dishes at a second-hand store and smash them into a garbage can together.

Provide Physical Support – You can certainly help your child in this respect if you live close by. The fatigue that accompanies grief is debilitating. In many cases your child is maintaining a full time job as well as keeping a home. Many have surviving children to care for as well. Help with laundry, cooking meals, shopping, running errands. But ask first. Having someone suddenly take over your household can only add to the stress.

Take the surviving children for a day or an afternoon. This will give your bereaved child some time. The grandchildren might enjoy it, too. This gives them an opportunity to be away from the constant sadness that is likely to permeate their home and to have a day with a good grandparent. When they are with you, if they want to talk about their dead sibling, by all means, practice your listening skills.

Physically Hold Your Child – We are willing to bet there are times when your child would love to crawl up on "mommy's" or "daddy's" lap to be comforted as in years past. Be aware of this and actually allow it in any way possible. Even a hand on an arm means a lot. The need to be held is stronger during tears or an especially hard time. Many times, your child may not be aware of wanting to be held, but you can take the initiative, for sons as well as daughters. The real benefit is that you feel you are doing something to help, not just sitting back helplessly watching your child suffer. It's perfectly all right to offer your lap as well as your hands, shoulders, heart and tears.

HOW TO LISTEN

Giving the Best Gift Possible

Few of us really know how to listen, but it's essential that you listen well if you're to help your child. Too often we think we're listening when what we're really doing is waiting for a break in the conversation so we can say something. That's not listening; that's shifting attention to ourselves.

If you're like the rest of us, you probably have a need to say something that will make it better or cheer up your child. And like me, you want her better now. Other than letting your child know of your love, there is nothing you can say. There are no words to take away the pain. Perhaps the most helpful thing you can say is simply, "I know it must feel that way for you."

If you think of someone you really like, you will probably realize that person is a good listener. Nothing pleases us more than someone who listens to us and lets us know what we are saying is important. It is not an inborn talent. You have to learn to listen. You can't fake it.

It's vital to want to listen. If you think your child is unnecessarily repeating a story, or talking about emotions that make you uncomfortable, then you are judging, not listening. Listen, not because you want to hear a story for the tenth time, but because you know your child needs to be listened to.

Hand in hand with wanting to listen, you must be committed to the task of listening. You can't simply sit there with one ear partly tuned to what's being said and the other to the television. Your child needs two attentive ears and an attentive body.

Another listening skill is patience. It takes patience to hear your child's stories, feelings and questions again and again. It sometimes takes an effort NOT to say, "You told me that before," or dismiss what's being said with your inattention. It's crucial that you allow your child to talk out feelings repeatedly.

If you feel yourself getting in a hurry to get the conversation over with, if you have an urge to suggest an immediate solution to the problem or tell your child how to think or feel, catch yourself. You are not listening.

Part of listening is not filling every silence. Most of us are uncomfortable with silence. When your child sees that you are there and will listen even to the silent moments, you encourage more sharing and closeness. Listening says you care, you are there and want to help.

Listening can happen any place, but the most likely spots are at your home, your child's home or on the telephone. However, some great listening has been done on walks, in shopping malls and in restaurants. If you are in the midst of a sharing time and there is an interruption, suggest something like, "Let's go into the next room where we can talk better."

When your child begins talking, try to sit close. Remember how bereaved parents have the need to sit on mommy's or daddy's lap? Try to be close enough to touch or hold your child. An arm around a shoulder, or holding hands can mean a lot.

Be attentive to what is being said. Lean toward your child. Have direct eye contact. Literally hang on every word. Don't drum your fingers on the table or look at your watch. Don't let your behavior be distracting. When you listen attentively you are saying, non-verbally, "I am listening and I am with you."

Frequently reflect back what you hear your child saying. For instance:

Child: "I can't believe Johnnie rode his motorcycle over that embankment. I hope he didn't suffer before he died." **You:** "It seems impossible and you're worried that he felt a lot of pain."

OR
Child: "I was too busy with work. I didn't pay enough attention to him. I should have known he was going to take his own life."
You: "It sounds like you're blaming yourself for Mike's suicide."

Don't parrot. Don't simply repeat the words. Try to sense what your child is feeling. This says you are really listening and lets your child see things from a different perspective.

Sometimes you need to ask questions to be sure of what your child is saying, or to encourage more talk. When you ask a question, give your child time to think and respond, then really listen.

Don't say: "Did you talk to Mike's doctor today? You look like he gave you bad news. You know it wasn't your fault." Do say: "What did Mike's doctor have to say?" (Then listen.)

At times you can say things or make suggestions to help your child, but be careful. Listen before being directive. Remember, your suggestions, advice and comments should rise out of your child's needs, not yours.

Child: "What should I do with Mike's clothes and things?"
You: "They're precious to you and you don't want to just toss them." **Child:** "Right. I want them to go to people who loved Mike." **You:** "I'm wondering who you think of first." **Child:** "I think I'll keep what I want, then let family and Mike's friends go through everything and take what they want."

When you're on track, the response you're likely to get will be something similar to, "*Right.*" Your child is recognizing that you actually hear what is being said. You are saying it's okay to have feelings. You are not judging. You are giving your child permission to think and feel. You are opening the door for feelings to be shared, and your child knows it is safe to share with you. These are precious moments.

A good listener listens more than talks. Because the techniques of effective listening may be new to you, or because you are under stress, check yourself occasionally to be sure you are not talking too much.

Listen with a third ear. Listen for what your child is saying behind the words. Listen for what is not said. Try to detect what is felt deep inside. Pay attention to posture. Do body and words fit? In other words, listen between the lines.

Your child may be hesitant to talk about some thoughts or feelings. Let it be known that no matter what it might be, no matter how "terrible," it's okay to talk about it. Remember, your child will feel better, you will be a trusted friend and your child will be more real and honest with you.

Actively listening is the most valuable gift you can give. Talking out loud is absolutely essential for bereaved parents. Listening will help more than anything you do. If, however, you are really uncomfortable with your child's pain, and don't want to hear what your child feels or thinks, then recommend a bereaved parent's group or grief counselor who will listen. Don't place more guilt on yourself because of your own pain. But first, give it a try. You have nothing to lose and a lot to gain by listening.

Read some books on listening. A good one is ***Parent Effectiveness Training,*** by Thomas Gordon. And remember – it's important for you to share your feelings, too. You won't always be listening. You'll be sharing with your child what's going on inside of you, how you feel, what you think. Hopefully, there will be some good talks for all of you.

FOR
GRANDFATHERS

If you are a bereaved grandfather, you may have special difficulty grieving the loss of a grandchild for two reasons. First, your grief is minimized by people who don't consider a grandfather/grandchild relationship to be very significant. Secondly, like most men, you have probably been taught to keep your feelings inside.

When a child dies, the concern of others is first for the mother, then the father and occasionally for the grandmother. Rarely do people recognize that you, too, are hurting. When you weep or express pain, even among family and friends, your behavior may be questioned. You may feel embarrassed. A grandfather isn't expected to be upset. He is expected to concern himself with his children and his wife.

The second, most important factor that prevents grandfathers from grieving is conditioning – how you were brought up and how society tells you to behave. There is much talk today about the "new male," and many bereaved fathers are of that breed, but most grandfathers are not. Conditioning is deeply set, and while men and women feel the same emotions when they lose someone they love, as a man you probably feel you can't cry, lament your loss or turn to others for support as women can.

Growing up, you learn from observing your father and other men. Teachers, relatives and friends condition you to ways of behaving in our society. Ordinarily, this works. However, when you experience a deep loss or other emotional stress, this conditioning can prohibit you from grieving in a healthy way.

Bill Schatz, bereaved father and writer on male grief, identifies four learned roles that prevent healthy grieving:
> Macho Man
> Protector
> Provider
> Self-Sufficient Man

The idea of **Macho Man** begins in early childhood with such sayings as "Big boys don't cry," and is reinforced throughout life. Movies, television, and advertising are big contributors to Macho Man. Therefore, when you feel sadness at losing an important person, your throat may tighten, tears may come to your eyes, but conditioning won't let you cry. You push the tears down inside, get busy caring for others, overwork, and sometimes turn to alcohol for relief.

As **Protector**, you are expected to protect your wife, children, and others close to you. When someone you love dies, failure can haunt you. It was impossible to protect the one you loved from death, and it's impossible to protect your grieving family from pain and sadness.

As **Provider**, you are expected to work so you go back to work almost immediately after the death. There you meet other men who don't know what to say to you. Those men, conditioned as you have been, expect you to go on with your work, keeping a "stiff upper lip." You can feel isolated. One grandfather told of returning to work after the funeral and seeing people duck down corridors to avoid having to greet him.

This is a time when you are apt to experience difficulty concentrating, a lack of physical energy, and the depression that comes with normal grief. You struggle to get through the day. You're tired, confused, and you feel alone. If you are retired, you may no longer go out of the home to work, but the sense of **Provider** is still strong, and your reactions are likely to be the same.

All your life you are taught to stand on your own two feet. You become the **Self-Sufficient Man**. You are taught not to ask for help. When you need support, your conditioning won't allow you to cry or talk about your grief.

This kind of self-sufficiency can keep you from reaching out to family and friends for support, and can also prevent you from joining a bereavement group, or from seeking the professional help you may need.

All this makes it extremely difficult for grandfathers to share grief. But there are ways for grandfathers to grieve. Expressing emotion is not weakness, but strength. Big boys do cry (just look at the losers after the Super Bowl), and what others think is not important. Expressing the emotions of grief is necessary for healthy resolution.

Learn to cry again. If you can't cry in front of others, do it alone. Go to the cemetery and cry. Cry in the privacy of your bedroom. Cry in the shower. Do what you need to get the tears out.

Exercise is a good release of energy created by emotions. Try walking, running, bicycling, swimming, etc. It's wise to check with your doctor first and to start slow on any exercise program.

Find a group for bereaved people. Grandparents are always welcome at a Compassionate Friends' meeting or a general bereavement group. Attend a meeting, even if just once, and you will find you are not alone. You are not required to say anything to the group if you do not want to talk.

As a grieving, caring Grandfather, direct your anger and frustration at things, not people.

> Walk, run, exercise
>
> Beat a bed with a dish towel
>
> Write out your feelings in a journal

Let your family know that although you may express your grief differently, you are grieving. You do care.

Know that suppressed emotions can cause physical problems. Don't let yourself be boxed into unhealthy behaviors just because society says so. An emotionally complete person experiences all his emotions, not just the socially acceptable ones.

You can do much to help your son or son-in-law. Because you both may have been taught to be stoic and suppress your emotions, you can help each other in ways only one man can help another.

Typically, two hurting men tip-toe around each other pretending that everything is fine. Don't let this happen. Take the initiative and tell him how you are feeling. Tell him how you miss your grandchild and how you hurt. Encourage him to share his feelings with you. Grieve together, cry together. Let go of old patterns. You will both be better emotionally and physically for it. And equally important, you will cement a bond between yourself and your bereaved children.

> *Once I saw a grown man cry*
> *"Now there goes a man with feelings!" said I.*
> *He was strong, able, quite well-built,*
> *With muscles, gray hair and charm to the hilt.*
>
> *I moved toward him slowly and said, "What's wrong?"*
> *The look he gave me was tear-filled and long.*
> *"I cry for a child. My grandchild has died."*
> *So I sat beside him and two grown men cried.*

GRANDPARENTS
AND
HOLIDAYS

During the holidays we sometimes feel we need to be all things to all our children. We want to share in the joy and excitement of our children with complete families. For our bereaved children we want to understand, empathize, and above all, be aware of the special difficulty holidays bring for them. We are caught in the middle of our children – a happy family on one side, a sad one on the other. In addition, we have our own pain. All this sounds impossible. None of us can do the impossible. None of us should try.

Remember when your children were young, and one was sick and needed special attention? You gave the extra attention and love that was needed. This didn't mean you loved the sick child more than the others; it simply meant that the sick one needed you more at that time. So it is with your bereaved child. That child is experiencing great pain and needs special attention.

To help yourself as well as your bereaved children, consider changing some holiday traditions. Have a buffet instead of a sit-down dinner, or put the decorations in a different place or another room. Recognize that the holiday is different and painful this year, and lean into that painful difference by making obvious changes.

Enlist your other children's aid in helping your bereaved child during the holiday. These children are grieving, too, of course. Remind them that while it may be somewhat uncomfortable for them to talk about a child who is dead, it is much more difficult to be the parent of a dead child and not hear the name mentioned. Remind them, too, that all of you need some normalcy. It's all right to laugh and enjoy. It's all right to hug and cry. Grief and happiness are things you share as a family, during holidays or every day.

Think of ways to remember and honor your grandchild in your family celebration. Suggest that each person say how they miss the child, or talk about a certain thing they remember about him. You may want to light a candle or display a picture in a place of honor to commemorate the life of this special youngster.

The holidays will never be the same again for you and your family. There will always be a child or children missing. It will not always be as difficult and painful as it is the first few years, but you will never again have the old normal. Instead, all of you will be creating a new normal.

SEXUAL
INTIMACY

As liberated as our society claims to be, talking about sexual feelings is still taboo. Oh yes, we can joke about sex and talk about academic aspects of it, but we still can't share our personal sexuality and needs.

Clarice Schultz, RN, in her audio tape, ***Sexual Adjustments of the Bereaved Parent,*** says that people need to be touched, hugged and cuddled. But in America, touching is seen as sexual, and sex as orgasmic. She says that Americans allow touching in only two situations: during sexual contact and by people licensed to touch – hairdressers, doctors, tailors, masseurs, etc. We might add NFL players following a touchdown.

As mature people, you have already established sexual patterns in your marriage. The problem arises if, in your grief, those past patterns don't feel right. One of you may need the closeness and intimacy that sex can bring. The other may want to be left completely alone. Both are normal reactions.

The secret to satisfying each other's needs is communication. Let your partner know of your needs. Don't assume your mate feels the same way you do, or, worse yet, assume that his or her need for sex ignores your grandchild's death. Your grandchild's death creates a lot of stress. Don't expect too much of yourself or your spouse.

Clarice says it well, "*Touching is one of the best therapies we can offer to one another. A hug or a pat on the shoulder, or holding someone can be one of the best helps. For the person who feels he has no center, being held can physically pull that center back in. For the person who does not want intimacy, hugging and caressing can give a sense of being loved and of worth. Hugging can be a stepping stone back to a deeper physical relationship.*"

One couple agreed to at least one two-minute hug every day. Later they shared that it improved everything. While you are grieving, sex can be a gentle stroking and caring that allows you to be part of each other. Like your bereaved children, you, too, need more touching, hugging and loving while you are sad. Some couples find it helpful to talk about how they met, how they came to fall in love and what they like about each other. This is tender talk and can be valuable in bringing you closer as you recall good and sometimes delightful memories.

GUILT

Guilt is so common we believe it deserves special attention. Almost every grieving person experiences guilt and grandparents are no exception. It's said that guilt, like depression, is anger turned inward. You may find it unacceptable to be angry at God, unacceptable to be angry at your bereaved child, unacceptable to even be angry at your grandchild for dying and leaving everyone in such pain. Therefore, you may turn your anger inside and blame yourself. Granted, your guilt isn't logical, but then, feelings aren't facts. It's all a part of the horrendous powerlessness that comes when death occurs.

Some of us have *survival guilt.* You may think, "I have experienced life. Why am I still living and my grandchild is dead?"

Another kind of guilt is *moral guilt.* It's the idea that your grandchild's death is a punishment for something you did. You may think, "I've tried to be a good person, why did this happen?" or, "I know this is my punishment for… " Believe me, this is not your punishment. What kind of God would kill a child to punish you?

There is even *geographic guilt.* You may feel guilty if you live far from your child and are not able to be there when needed. You can help with warm and loving phone calls and letters. Be sure to mention your grandchild. Remind yourself that you would be with your child if you could.

The most *devastating guilt* we experience comes when we are directly involved in the cause of the death. One couple's grandchild drowned in their swimming pool while they were babysitting. Another's grandchild died from a skateboard accident while he was visiting them. A grandfather was driving the car in which his infant granddaughter was killed. This is a shattering guilt and professional help may be needed.

Recovery guilt is very common. Your grief will probably begin to lessen sooner than your child's grief. Six months after Emily died, I began having good days. I actually felt good about some things. But I wasn't comfortable with feeling good. I didn't want my daughter to know I was feeling better. She was having a painful time just then. Foolishly, I felt I was betraying her by feeling better. I was afraid she might think I didn't love Emily if I weren't still hurting.

When Dorothy saw that I was not grieving as deeply as I had been, her reaction was totally the opposite of what I expected. She told me she was relieved she didn't have me to worry about.

It takes time and work to get through guilt. Identify, as clearly as possible, what it is you believe you are guilty of. Then ask yourself if your guilt is logical or not. Ask yourself if you did the best you could with the knowledge, tools, and abilities you had at the time. If you need to do this over and over, do it!

Guilt needs to be talked out. Find a non-judgmental person to talk to and talk to them repeatedly until you resolve your guilt. If talking is difficult for you, write out your guilt in a journal or a letter. Talk to yourself. Picture the person you believe you have wronged sitting across from you. Talk directly to that person. Talk out what happened.

For some of us, asking for forgiveness is the only answer. You can ask forgiveness from God, your deceased grandchild, your bereaved child or anyone you feel you've wronged. A talk with your clergy person may bring forgiveness. Ultimately, ***you have to forgive yourself.*** And finally, some of us find it helpful to simply wallow in guilt until we tire of it.

Very often, guilt and self-pity go hand-in-hand. If these are a permanent part of your life, you may want to take a serious look at what they get you. Usually, they're used to attract attention. You don't really need them. One grandmother found a great cartoon of two women sitting on a bench. One said to the other, *"You shouldn't wallow in self-pity, but it doesn't hurt to put your feet in it and swish 'em around for a few minutes."* Guilt and self-pity were such an ingrained part of this grandmother's life that she actually allowed herself 10 minutes every morning to do nothing but feel guilty and sorry for herself. When her 10 minutes were up, she imagined windshield wipers in front of her eyes, wiping away all the guilt and pity. Then if she felt those emotions at any other time of the day, out came the wipers and she refused to allow herself further wallowing.

True, this is a time when you have a right to "put your feet in and swish 'em around for a few minutes." Your grandchild has died, and everyone feels sad and hurt. Everyone thinks they could have done more. Everyone feels sorry for themselves, but it's unhealthy to stay in those feelings. Guilt and self-pity are unproductive behaviors. It accomplishes nothing to punish yourself for the rest of your life for something you can't change. Rather, you need to reserve as much energy as possible in order to help yourself and your bereaved children through this grief.

A DEEPER
RELATIONSHIP

Some grandparents have a deeper relationship than usual with their grandchildren. While not the biological parents, you reared the child as a parent would. You probably don't feel that you fit the role of bereaved parent or bereaved grandparent. The information on helping a bereaved child doesn't apply to you.

If you parented your grandchild, your grief is certainly as legitimate as the grief of a parent. Allow yourself to grieve as fully as you need to, and make no apologies for doing so.

FUTURE
GRANDCHILDREN

I was surprised when the first new grandbaby was expected after Emily died. I wasn't thrilled as I had been with other grandbabies. There was a part of me that was glad, but there was an even stronger part that wasn't happy at all. At times I actually resented the idea of a new infant. After talking to other grandparents, I found I wasn't the only one who reacted like this.

Unless your family had already experienced the death of a child, you probably found it hard to believe that children die. I had lost a child, and I, too, had become lulled into the idea that it can't happen to grandchildren. But now we all know that grandchildren die, too. With a new baby, we unconsciously fear it will happen again. We have been terribly hurt, and we don't want to be hurt again.

It helped me to recognize that my feelings about the new grandbaby had nothing to do with the child herself, but were caused by the pain of Emily's death. I told myself that my feelings were okay and would eventually go away. They did.

Sometimes subsequent grandbabies remind us of our dead grandchild. You may decide to let the new parents take the lead in discussing whether or not their baby looks like the deceased child. However, I readily talk with my bereaved daughter about how the new baby looks like Emily. Dorothy likes to see Emily reflected in other children in the family.

. . . AND THE GRIEF GOES ON

You learn to live without your grandchild, but there will always be the "might have beens."

For the rest of your life there will be times when you see that distant look in your bereaved child's eyes and know that thoughts of your grandchild are surfacing from the heart.

It's true that your child will live again without pain, and so will you.

But don't be surprised when...

> *Her hair was long and dark, with just a little*
> *Curl in the ends. Her eyes were big and blue and she just*
> *Couldn't stand still. She looked up at the older woman and*
> *Said, "I want chocolate, Grandma!" My heart sank.*
> *She reminded me so much of Emily.*
> *I stood there, aching, wishing*
> *That Emily was there with me waiting for her ice cream.*

It's been just a few years since my three-year old granddaughter died and I feel I have resolved my grief quite well, but every so often I see a little girl who reminds me of her, and it's all brought back in a rush.

> *God, how it hurts.*

It's been many years since my son was killed. Fortunately, the pain is only momentary when, occasionally, I see a little blond, brown-eyed boy. I know that someday I won't feel deep pain when I see a little girl who reminds me of Emily, but for now I just have to expect that I will hurt deeply at times.

The differences between the depth of pain is having worked through my grief in both cases and the passage of time. I tend to say, *Why am I feeling hurt after three years?* but then I have to remind myself that it hasn't been all that long. Emily wiggled herself deep into my heart in minutes, and she isn't going to leave it in three years. I know she will never leave it, but someday the searing pain will. I (and you) just have to be patient.

About the Author

Margaret Gerner is a bereaved parent and a bereaved grandparent. Her son, Arthur, was six years old when he was killed by an automobile in May, 1971. Her three-year-old granddaughter, Emily, died of an unknown liver ailment in August, 1982. She has seven surviving children.

In 1979 she founded the St. Louis Chapter of The Compassionate Friends. She continues to be involved with the group today and at one time edited both the St. Louis and national TCF newsletters.

Margaret has written extensively on parent and grandparent grief. At present she is a bereavement specialist for John Stygar and Son Funeral Directors in St. Louis, Missouri, and the director of the Chrysalis Center, a bereavement counseling and resource center for funeral directors. She publishes the Chrysalis newsletter for people in grief and writes for various funeral service periodicals. She holds a Masters degree in Social Work from the University of Missouri.

About the Illustrator

Vibrant, jewel-toned colors characterize the watercolors and pastels of Glenda Dietrich. Her artwork has been featured in books she has illustrated (*Goodbye My Child, Since My Brother Died* and *I Know I Made It Happen* from The Centering Corporation), in magazines such as The Upper Room and The Other Side, on book covers, and as illustrations and posters. View her artwork at www.Glendadietrich.com.

Other Helpful Resources

More Than Surviving: Caring for Yourself While You Grieve by Kelly Osmont
Grief: What It Is and What You Can Do by Joy and Marv Johnson
I Remember, I Remember - a keepsake journal by Enid Traisman
Not Just Another Day - families, grief and special days by Missy Lowery

Centering Corporation is a small, non-profit bereavement resource center.
Please call or write for a free catalog of available material.

Additional copies may be ordered from:
Centering Corporation
PO Box 4600
Omaha, NE 68104

Phone: 402-553-1200
Fax: 402-553-0507

Website: www.centering.org
Email: j1200@aol.com